THE   WILD   PARTY

DRAWINGS BY
ART SPIEGELMAN

THE

THE LOST CLASSIC BY

WILD

JOSEPH MONCURE MARCH

PARTY

PANTHEON BOOKS · NEW YORK

Published in the United States by Pantheon Books, a division of Random House, Inc., New York, and simultaneously in Canada by Random House of Canada Limited, Toronto. *The Wild Party* was originally published in 1928 by Pascal Covici. Copyright © 1928 by Pascal Covici, Publisher, Inc. Library of Congress Cataloging-in-Publication Data: *The Wild Party:* The lost classic by Joseph Moncure March; drawings by Art Spiegelman. p. cm. ISBN 0-679-42450-4 I. Spiegelman, Art. II. March, Joseph Moncure. PS3525.A58W5 1994 813'.52—dc20 94-11682. Manufactured in the United States of America. Book design: Art Spiegelman. Type design: Louise Fili / Art Spiegelman. Typesetting: Leah Lococo. Production: Robert Sikoryak.

2 4 6 8 9 7 5 3 1
First Edition

INTOXICATING RHYTHM

t was the spine that grabbed me. I'm like a drunk who is as attracted to bottles and their labels as to the liquid within. I mean, I once even bought a cookbook—a cookbook!—because of its binding. I get the same pleasure from used bookstores that an alcoholic finds in bars. Both places, though public, make room for feverish solitude and both allow unhealthy cravings to be filled to excess. And just like a drunk who won't touch, say, rye except as a last resort, I rarely stray toward the poetry shelves; so it's peculiar that I ever stumbled onto *The Wild Party*. It was the twenties typography on the spine that first made me pick up the book in the early seventies, and it was a perfunctory frontispiece by Reginald Marsh that made me linger.

Anyway, my fetishistic interest in the trappings led me to discover the poem itself. Joseph Moncure March's *Wild Party* is a hard-boiled, jazz-age tragedy told in syncopated rhyming couplets. It has the mnemonic tenacity, if not the wholesomeness, of a nursery rhyme, and to read it once is to get large shards of it permanently lodged in the brain.

Several years after falling in love with the poem, I met William Burroughs. The conversation didn't catch fire until, somehow, I asked if he'd ever heard of *The Wild Party*. Burroughs had first read the book in 1938, when he was a graduate student at Harvard. He hadn't seen it in over thirty years. *"The Wild Party?"* he mused. ". . . It's the book that made me want to be a writer." His eyes unfocused and he began to recite, in a twanging drawl:

> *"Queenie was a blonde, and her age stood still,*
> *And she danced twice a day in vaudeville."*

He went on for quite a while, as if he could conjure up the whole poem from memory, all the way to the abrupt last lines:

> *"The door swung open*
> *And the cops rushed in."*

In an admiring introduction to the first edition of the book, Louis Untermeyer raised a question in my mind by admitting that "I haven't the faintest idea whether it is good or bad poetry. In fact, I'm not sure that it is poetry at all." So I asked Burroughs, who set me straight: "Of course it's poetry. It rhymes."

The Wild Party is closer to "Frankie and Johnny" than to *Tristan and Iseult*, but March had been a protégé of Robert Frost's at Amherst, and knew his way around villanelles as well as around speakeasies. It owes as much to the language and sizzle of tabloids, to the lyrics and rhythms of hot jazz and to the close-ups and cuts of silent films as it does to any earlier narrative verse other than off-color limericks. The twenty-six-year-old March improvised the poem, a few lines a day, over the summer of 1926, soon after quitting *The New Yorker*, where he had been the fledgling magazine's first managing editor (or "Jesus" as the staff came to christen the post). He decided to make his way as a poet—a career choice underwritten by an indulgent father.

The poem was considered too hot to publish until 1928, when a limited edition of seven hundred and fifty copies—the one with the Marsh frontispiece—was released by Pascal Covici. (March and Marsh, I eventually learned, had become friends while seated in alphabetical proximity at prep school.) The book became a succès de scandale and got banned in Boston. March immediately followed up with *The Set-Up*, the story of a washed-up black boxer, which is similar in structure to *The Wild Party*, but without its sexual charge. *The Set-Up* made the *Times* best-seller list, and March moved to Hollywood, where he worked on screenplays throughout the next decade. Most notably, he collaborated on the story and provided dialogue for *Hell's Angels*, the 1930 talkie that made Jean Harlow—the embodiment of Queenie—a star.

March became a writer of documentaries for the State Department and a feature writer for *The New York Times Magazine*. He died in 1977, his two major works out-of-print and under-appreciated, though the poems have had a ghostly half-life on film: a deracinated 1949 movie adaptation of *The Set-Up*, directed by Robert Wise, remains one of the world's great noir boxing films; a 1975 Merchant-Ivory film called *The Wild Party*, starring Raquel Welch and James Coco, unsuccessfully conflated March's poem with the Fatty Arbuckle scandal.

A self-censored version of *The Wild Party* and *The Set-Up*, accompanied by a short memoir, was published in 1968. In a misguided attempt to avoid offense, many of the ethnic references in the poem were removed. This current edition follows the original text, considering it a perfect picture of its time. My own desire to illustrate *The Wild Party* grows from something beyond a yen for the innocent hedonism of the boop-a-doop and vo-de-oh-do twenties, although I confess to a powerful nostalgia for all decades that precede my birth. After all, we've already lived through each decade of the century at least twice. In this Postmodern moment we can see them all simultaneously—the austerity of the thirties, the Genocide of the forties, the platform shoes of the seventies—while we plummet into the millennium, as if we were drowning and watching our past flash before us.

Maybe it's March's perfectly pitched tone of bewildered innocence curdled into worldly cynicism that resonates so well in our nineties. March's "lost" generation saw civilization unglued by The War to End All Wars. Our "foundering" generation has recently seen the End of History. His generation swilled bathtub gin and had a wild party. Our generation gulps Prozac—or gets lost in used bookstores—while waiting for the cops to rush in.

—art spiegelman

THE
WILD
PARTY

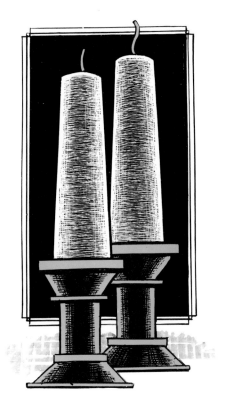

PART I

1

Queenie was a blonde, and her age stood still,

And she danced twice a day in vaudeville.

Grey eyes.

Lips like coals aglow.

Her face was a tinted mask of snow.

What hips—

What shoulders—

What a back she had!

Her legs were built to drive men mad.

And she did.

She would skid.

But sooner or later they bored her:

Sixteen a year was her order.

They might be blackguards;

They might be curs;

They might be actors; sports; chauffeurs—

She never inquired

Of the men she desired

About their social status, or wealth:

She was only concerned about their health.

True:

She knew:

There was little she hadn't been through.

And she liked her lovers violent, and vicious:

Queenie was sexually ambitious.

So:

Now you know.

A fascinating woman, as they go.

She lived at present with a man named Burrs

Whose act came on just after hers.

A clown

Of renown:

Three-sheeted all over town.

He was comical as sin;

Comical as hell;

A gesture—a grin,

And the house would yell,

Uproarious:

He was glorious!

So from the front. People in the wings

Saw him and thought of other things

Coldly—

Most coldly:

Many would say them boldly,

Adding in language without much lace

They'd like to break his god-damned face.

Ask why?

They might be stuck:

They would like to, just for luck.

But these were men, for the greater part.

A woman would offer him up her heart

Throbbing,

On a platter:

He could bite it, and it wouldn't matter.

As long as he kissed, and held her tight,

And gave her a fairly hectic night.

Which he could,

And would.

A man these women understood!

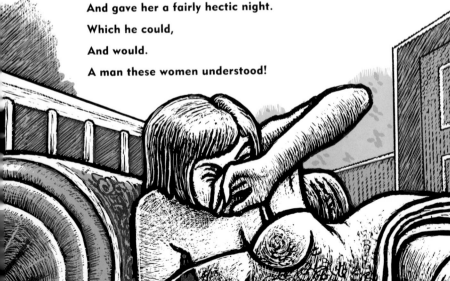

Oh, yes—Burrs was a charming fellow:

Brutal with women, and proportionately yellow.

Once he had been forced into a marriage.

Unlucky girl!

She had a miscarriage

Two days later. Possibly due

To the fact that Burrs beat her

   with the heel of a shoe

Till her lips went blue.

For a week her brother had great fun

Looking for Burrs with a snub-nosed gun:

At the end of which time, she began to recover;

And Burrs having vanished, the thing blew over.

Just a sample

For example:

One is probably ample.

2

Studio;

Bedroom;

Bath;

Kitchenette:

Furnished like a third act passion set:

Oriental;

Sentimental;

They owed two months on the rental.

Pink cushions,
Blue cushions: overlaid
With silk: with lace: with gold brocade.
These lay propped up on a double bed
That was covered with a Far East tapestry spread.

Chinese dragons with writhing backs:
Photographs caught to the wall with tacks:
Their friends in the profession,
Celebrities for the impression—
("So's your old man—Isidore."
"Faithfully—Ethel Barrymore.")

On a Chinese lacquer tray there stood a
Gong with tassels, and a brass Buddha.
Brass candlesticks.
Orange candles.
An Art vase with broken handles,
Out of which came an upthrusting
Of cherry blossoms that needed dusting.

Books?

Books?

My god! You don't understand.

They were far too busy living first-hand

For books.

Books!

True,

On the table there lay a few

Tattered copies of a magazine,

Confessional;

Professional;

That talked of their friends on the stage and screen.

A Victrola with records

Just went to show

Queenie's Art on the man two floors below.

Being a person of little guile,

He had lent them to her, for just awhile.

Believe it or not—

All this for a smile!

A grand piano stood in the corner
With the air of a coffin waiting for a mourner.

The bath was a horrible give-away.
The floor was dirty:
The towels were grey.
Cups, saucers,
Knives, plates,
Bottles, glasses
In various states
Of vileness, fought for precarious space in
The jumbled world beneath the basin.

The basin top was the temporary home
Of a corkscrew, scissors,
And a brush and comb.
In the basin bowel
Was a Pullman towel
Vividly wrought with red streaks
From Queenie's perfect lips and cheeks.
Behind one faucet, in a stain of rust,
Spattered with talcum powder and dust,
A razor blade had lived for weeks.
Beside it was stuck a cigarette stub.

And the tub?
Oh—never mind the tub!

On the door-knob there hung a pair
Of limp stockings, and a brassiere
Too soiled to wear.

Of the bedroom,
Nothing much to be said.
It had a bureau:
A double bed
With one pillow, and white spread.
Their trunks: boxes.
A chair.
The walls were white and bare.
Only occasional guests slept there:
Queenie and Burrs, preferring air,
Slept with the Chinese dragons instead.

Sunday noon:

Broiling hot.

Queenie woke up feeling shot.

She lay stretched out on the crumpled bed

Naked: slim arms above her head.

She stared at the ceiling;

She stared at her feet;

She stared at the clock,

And she cursed the heat

Faintly:

Quaintly.

She looked exquisite; saintly.

Burrs was up,

Ugly; silent;

Unshaven;

    dressed in a pair of violent

Pink pyjamas, badly crumpled.

His eyes were pouched.

His hair was rumpled.

He sat brooding like a captive satyr

Over a cup and a percolator.

He was gross;

Morose.

The Sunday Tabloid spread before him

Rather unusually well supplied

With murder,

Rape,

And suicide,

Left him cold: unsatisfied.

Even the comics seemed to bore him.

Queenie lifted her head
A trifle from the bed.
"Burrsie!" she piped.
Her voice was pitched
In a fretful key.
His mouth twitched:
He was dangerously still,
By enormous power of will.
Her eyes filled with a martyred look:
She registered grief, and her voice shook.
"Burrsie!"
Sharply—
"Well?" he inquired.
"Burrsie! Queenie is oh, so tired!"

His teeth snapped.
He was glittering-eyed.
For a moment or so he could not decide
Whether it would be best to throttle
Or brain this woman with a nearby bottle.
A woman who slept
Like a corpse under sod,
And woke up tired!
Almighty God!

His nerves jangled.
He saw red.

He said nothing: but Queenie did,

From the region of the bed,

Peevishly:

"Burrsie! Pour out a cup for me!"

Said she.

"The hell I will, you lazy slut!

Do you think you're the Prince of Wales,

Or what?"

Tense

Silence,

Foreboding sudden violence.

Queenie rolled up on to her side.

She looked Burrs over, narrow-eyed.

Her eyebrows rose

On a vicious slant:

Her mouth and chin grew adamant.

Burrs was afraid—

Already routed.

He tried bluster.

"Well!" he shouted,

Glaring:

But she simply lay there

Staring.

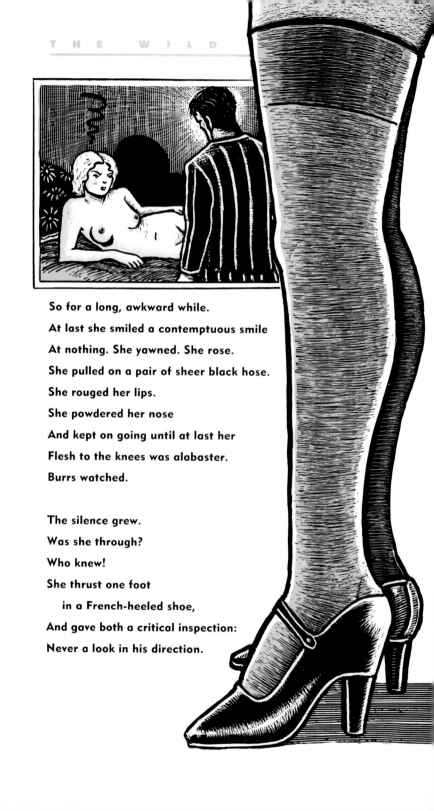

So for a long, awkward while.
At last she smiled a contemptuous smile
At nothing. She yawned. She rose.
She pulled on a pair of sheer black hose.
She rouged her lips.
She powdered her nose
And kept on going until at last her
Flesh to the knees was alabaster.
Burrs watched.

The silence grew.
Was she through?
Who knew!
She thrust one foot
   in a French-heeled shoe,
And gave both a critical inspection:
Never a look in his direction.

The silence chilled his brain.

"Queenie!"

Silence.

Again:

"Queenie!—Hell!"

He was stubborn now:

He'd make her talk, no matter how!

He set his teeth,

Swallowed his pride;

Rose:

Slunk over:

Crouched at her side.

"Queenie!"

He seized her arm; shook it.

She may have been pleased,

But she didn't look it.

Her eyes flashed:

No truce!

She wrenched her arm loose.

Up she leapt, white faced.

He lunged:

His arms went around her waist:

They tightened: they locked:

They crushed her thin.

For a moment, she writhed;

Then she gave in.

He pulled her backwards,

And her soft, slim

Body flew down and covered him.

His face was pressed

Deep in her breast.

She loosened.

She waited.

She lay still,

Giving his hands and lips their will.

She was cold as ice, all through it:

She had him now,

And she knew it.

His heart quickened:

His breath thickened.

She covered his mouth with a kiss like flame;

And he quivered; and he gasped;

And he almost came.

Now,
Swift as a snake,
She shifted.

Her shoulders rose.
Her arm lifted.
Down she struck.

His tight embrace
Gave. His hands covered his face.
She leapt up; fled, with hard laughter.
Bleeding at the mouth,
He rushed after.

"You rotten bitch!
I'll fix you yet!"

She grabbed a knife from the kitchenette,
And a brown bottle with a whisky label:
Then dodged
Swiftly
Around the table.

They paused: watched:
Animal-eyed,
Furious,
From either side.
Her face was white as though newly plastered.

"You touch me—
I'll kill you, you filthy bastard!"

The threat was banal,
But her tone lent it
A quality that showed she meant it.

A pause.

"Well—?"

It was over.

"My sweetie's bats—

But I love her!"

Said Burrs drily.

He smiled wryly.

He was wily.

Queenie shrugged, and took the cue.

"Aw, nuts—and to hell with you!"

Was her not too sentimental retort.

"Come on," urged Burrs: "be a sport!

Go on, Cutie—drop the knife!

Let's call it quits.

I like my life!"

"Yeah?" said Queenie: "I wouldn't choose it.

And once for all, I'll tell you what:

The next time you call me a lazy slut,

If I find a knife, I'll damn well use it!—

Kick that idea around till you lose it!"

Having delivered herself of this,

She gave him a condescending kiss.

She took a cracked cup from the shelf:

Rattled the percolator;

Helped herself.

Sat,

Sipped;

Perfect lipped,

Legs crossed:

At ease: engrossed.

Beautiful.

There was a lull.

Peace.

But her face was still white,

And her eyes flickered with angry light.

At last she gave an odd

Double nod.

She raised her handsome head;

She said:

"Burrsie, I think we're about due

For a party:

Don't you?"

Said Burrs: "I do!

My god! I haven't been really tight

For a week!

Let's ask the gang to-night!"

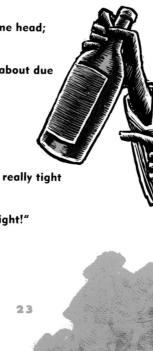

23

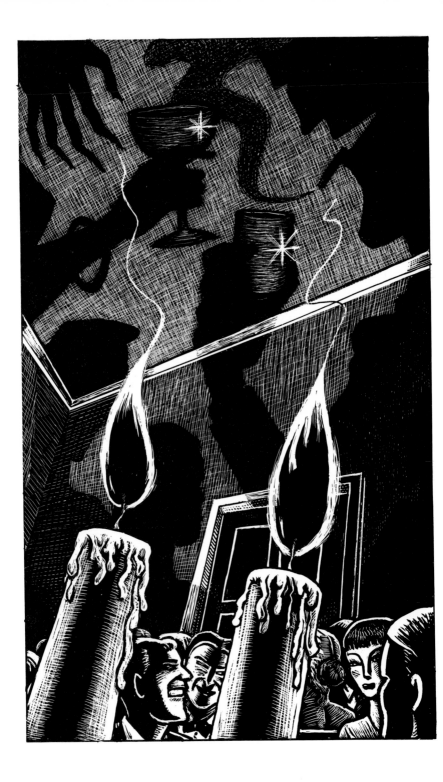

PART II

1

The gang was there when midnight came.

The studio was lit by candle-flame;

Dim: mysterious: shrouded.

Unbidden shadow-guests swarmed

About the room. They huddled crowded

In every corner; raised deformed

Ungainly shoulders, hideous, tall

Necks and heads against the wall.

Enormous blurred hands kept stealing

Spider-like, across the ceiling;

Crossing with sharp, prismatic masses

Of light from swaying spectre glasses.

The flames flickered:

The shadows leapt:

They rushed forward boldly;

Swept

Triumphant

Across white faces:

Wavered, retreated;

Turned, defeated,

And shrank back to darker places.

The party was getting under way
Stiffly, slowly.

The way they drank was unholy.
They hovered around the glass-filled tray
Ravenously,
Like birds of prey.
White, intense;
With mask-like faces
Frozen in rigid, gay grimaces.
They chattered and laughed
Stony-eyed:
Impatient:
Hasty:
Preoccupied.

They drank swiftly, as though they might
Drop dead before they were properly tight.

Christ,
What a crew!
Take a look at Madelaine True;
Her eyes slanted. Her eyes were green;
Heavy-lidded; pouched: obscene.
Eyes like a snake's:
Like a stagnant pool
Filled with slime.

Her mouth was cruel:
A scar
In red,
That had recently opened and bled.

Her body was marvellous:
A miracle had fused it:
The whole world had seen it—
And a good part had used it.
People bought their seats in advance
For fifteen dollars,
Glad of the chance
To see her dance.

Women adored her.
Less often, a man:
And the more fool he—
She was Lesbian.

Then Jackie:
Perfectly formed of face,
Slim, elegant,
Full of grace:
Leaving a subtle trail of scent
Floating behind him as he went.
A soft-shoe dancer
With a special act.
New York, or Paris—
His house was packed.

He had two cars.
He had been behind bars
For theft, public nuisance, rape:
Once extra for trying escape.
Too bad?
Nonsense!
He was fun.
A good sport:
The only son
Of some unheard-of preacher father
Who had kicked him out as too much bother.
Of course—
(The Black Horse)
His hips were jaunty,
And his gestures too dextrous.
A versatile lad!
He was ambisextrous.

By contrast—Eddie:

A short, squat brute,

Gorilla-like: hirsute:

With eyes deep set,

A nose battered

Flat on one side,

And teeth scattered.

The bones about his cheeks and eyes

Protruded grimly, oversize.

A boxer, you'd guess—

And right.

The man could certainly fight.

Aggressive; fast;

Punishment-proof :

Each hand held a kick like a mule's hoof.

He might have been champion—

He had the cunning:

But drink had put him out of the running.

Away from the ring, he was easy-going;

Good-natured—if sober—

And given to blowing.

But after he'd had his tenth Scotch,

A man to be careful of

And watch:

And when he was mixing gin and rum—

A man to keep well away from.

His woman at present was Mae.
She was blonde, and slender, and gay:
A passionate flirt,
So dumb that it hurt,
And better for night than for day.

Behold the Brothers d'Armano:
Otherwise, Oscar and Phil.
They sang:
They played the piano:
They functioned together with skill.
They lisped.
Their voices were shrill.
They were powdered,
Rouged,
Sleek of hair:
They must have worn
Pink silk underwear.

They clung together with arms laced
Each about the other's waist:
Stood around in anguished poses.
They rated
A shower of paper roses;
Lavender lights,
And the stink of joss.
Suffering Moses,
What a loss!

Watch Dolores:
Dark, tall,
Slim,
Wrapped in a Spanish shawl;
With a Spanish comb making a flare
Of crimson against her smooth, black hair.
A singer
Without a voice:
But she rode in a Rolls-Royce.
She made herself up, and out, to be
Of Spanish aristocracy.
(As a matter of fact,
If one only knew,
She was somewhat Negro
And a great deal Jew.)
In each eye lurked
What she thought was a dagger;
And she walked with a slink
Mixed with a swagger.
She was swell to sleep with.
Her toe-nails were scarlet.
She looked like—and had been—
A Mexican harlot.

There were others, of course:
A dozen or so.
Sally,
With Butter and Eggs in tow—
He had seen her first two nights ago
In the chorus of a summer musical show.

And the usual two
Loud Jew
Theatrical managers stood engrossed
Bewailing high production cost.
Each of them had suffered most.
In twenty minutes both had lost
The sum of sixty million dollars—
With gestures:
After which they sighed,
And drank
Panting:
Tragic-eyed:
Mopping at sadly wilted collars.

Nadine:

Mae's kid sister.

Fourteen:

No man had kissed her.

Excitement made her wide-eyed:

She was so thrilled to be there

She could have died!

She was quite pretty

And she looked older.

She knew only

What had been told her.

And of course, Burrs:

Natty in grey,

With a breath you could smell a yard away:

Putting his better foot foremost

And trying to be the perfect host.

The rest were simply repetitions

Of the more notorious. Slim editions:

Less practised; less hardened:

Less vicious; less strong:

Just a nice crowd trying to get along.

But to-night, Queenie surpassed them all.

Exquisite in black;

Radiant;

Tall;

With a face of ivory,

And blurred gold for hair:

She was something to kneel before, in prayer.

"My god, Queenie; you're looking swell!"

Quoth Queenie:

"I'm feeling slick as hell!"

2

The only one not on hand was Kate.

She was Queenie's red-headed running-mate.

She was rakish, and tall:

Slim-legged; slim-hipped:

Naughty of eye, and expressive-lipped.

Always in vogue:

Vicious,

Capricious:

A rogue—

But her manner was gay, and delicious.

She could make a Baptist preacher choke

With laughter over a dirty joke.

A touch of her flesh would drive you fey.

She could pull you in

To a state of sin

So fast it would take your breath away;

And you'd love it, and beg her to let you stay.

She had wrecked more homes

With lust's delight

Than most women could have

With dynamite.

She was cute,

Lecherous:

Lovable,

Treacherous:

And about as healthy as a cobra's bite.

"Where the hell is that dirty bum?"

Said Queenie: "She swore to God she'd come!"

At which point—

Bang! on the door.

"Come in!"

For answer, came only a high-pitched,

Thin

Laugh

Cut in half

By a scuffle outside.

Silence.

"Come in!"

The door sprang wide;

And there stood Kate,
    with a man by her side:

Both posing Heroic;
    mock-dignified.

"Ta-da!" sang Kate, clarion-toned:
"Well, Ladies
And what came with you," she droned—
"Meet what brought me in a sea-going hack:
The Boy Friend—Mister—Mister—
Black!
That's Queenie.
This's Burrs.
Tha's Jackie—Am I right?
My god! There's Mae!
'Lo, Mae!—I'm tight!"

Queenie came forward.
As she came, she ran her
Eye over Black in professional manner.
He was tall; dark; heavy of shoulder:
A possible twenty-five,
No older.
Quietly, even soberly dressed;
But perfectly groomed—a habit, one guessed.
He was carelessly straight.
His eyes were bright.
His face was tanned, and his smile was white.
His features were sharply cut
And clean:
He looked sporting: he looked keen.

He made you think of squash-rackets;

Polo; and yachting;

And dinner-jackets.

And he had that air of poise without pose

That only a well-bred person shows.

She paused for a second.

She looked askance

At Burrs:

A swift, narrow-eyed glance.

She smiled a smile

As sharp as a file

For the fraction of a while.

Again that odd

Slight double nod.

The spurs

For Burrs!

Just what she'd wanted!

He'd try to rough her,

The bastard?

 Well, now she'd make him suffer!

She had planned this party to put him on the rack;

And she'd do it by making a play for Black!

Her grey eyes widened:

They grew dim.

Doubtfully, shyly, she smiled at him.

"How do you do, Mr. Black," said she:
"We're rather informal here,
As you see.
It was sweet of you to come, I think.
Burrsie—mix Mr. Black a drink."

Black said something polite: astonished.
Then:
"Please don't think me rude
If I stare—
But—your hair—!"

"Listen to me, kid!" Kate admonished:
"Keep away from that blond-headed vamp:
She was wise to herself
When your ears were damp!"

"I haven't a bit of doubt," said Black.

He grinned at Queenie,
And she smiled back—

But with eyes dark: engrossed:
As though she saw a ghost.

Her lashes drooped; made a violet stain
Under each eye, like shadows of pain.
She held it a second,

Then seemed to recover.

It was deftly done—
And it got over.

Black said nothing, but his clear eyes took
On a gentle, understanding look.
Poor Child! Relentless Life had used
Her Brutally, and left her Bruised!
And beautiful—
God!
She might have been
Some legendary faery queen!

She moved off;
Left him staring after.
Kate burst out in sarcastic laughter.

"Well!

My God!

After all!

Queenie takes the brass-lined shawl!

My God, though: hasn't she got the gall,

Making a play for you that way!"

"What do you mean?" said Black:

"What play?"

"Say, kid—I wasn't born yesterday!

I like you, kid;

And I know I'm tight,

But I know what I'm talkin' about, all right!

An' let me tell you—she'll get hers

If she doesn't watch her step with Burrs!

See?

Let her be!

I've told you—now take it from me!"

Black said nothing, but he thought hard.

So she lived with Burrs!

He was somewhat jarred.

He looked Burrs over, and he liked his looks

About as well as a fish likes hooks.

So this was the man of her choosing?

Amusing!

His smile grew knowing:

His drink grew small:

Just a good-looking harlot, after all!

3

The candles sputtered: their flames were gay;

And the shadows leapt back out of the way.

The party began to get going.

The laughter rang shriller:

The talk boomed louder:

The women's faces showed flushed through powder;

And the men's faces were glowing.

The room was hung with streamers of smoke.

It billowed; curled:

Swung; swirled:

Poured towards the candle flames

And broke.

Eyes flashed,

Glistened:

Everyone talked:

Few listened.

Crash!

A glass smashed;

And a woman swore,

Shrank back

Abashed.

On the bed sat a girl,

Alone.

White: aloof:

Like stone.

Her mouth was a crimson velvet petal,

Her hair was beaten from gun-metal.

Her eyes were deeply set

In shadows of violet.

And she sat with never a motion,

Like a nun wrapped in devotion.

Hungrily Madelaine True eyed her:

Slowly she crossed:

Sank down beside her:

Softly she let a hand sink

On this girl's hand.

The girl did not shrink:

She did not speak:

She did not stir.

She sat staring at a shadow blur

That hung like a web to the opposite wall.

Gently Madelaine's fingers slid

Upwards along her slender, small

Ivory arm.

The lace that hid

The girl's bosom, rose and quivered:

Her petal lips parted:

She shivered.

Slowly she drew her arm away:

She rose, and went towards the glass-filled tray.

Kate hailed Burrs like a long-lost brother,

And she left Black's side

To be a red-hot Mother.

Queenie saw her going:

She stopped the Vic,

And put on a record so blue it was sick.

She moved forward swiftly:

She stood before Black:

"Will you dance with me—

Until Kate comes back?"

And ever so shyly she smiled.

He blushed like a ten-year-old child,

And nodded, completely beguiled.

So dance they did,
And dance they could:
Queenie was a marvel,
And the boy was good.

Their step was dreamy,
    and slow,
And sweeping:
And their rhythm was enough
    to set you weeping.
They stood up straight,
    and slim, and tall—
None of your sexy stuff at all:
Queenie was clever:
You should have seen them:
She danced as though there
    were a sword between them.

But the music swerved.
It sank into deep
Soft murmurs, as though it were falling asleep.
Like a dream, the melody began to float
From a saxophone's low-pitched, husky throat:
And the rhythm whispered with the fierce unrest
Of a heart throbbing in a passionate breast.

Then Queenie stirred;
And the stir went through him;

And he shifted his arm,
And crushed her to him.
The shock of her softness
    stopped his breath.

Lights blurred:
The floor swam underneath.
And Queenie did more than her share:
She brushed his lips with her hair:
She arched inward:
She clung:
She pressed
Her body on his
    from knee to breast.

It was wonderfully timed.
About two steps more,
They'd have lost their balance
And fallen on the floor.
As it was, the music quavered:
Stopped.
They disengaged slowly:
Their arms dropped.
And she fed him a blurred,
    bewildered glance.
She smiled: she whispered:
"Our first dance!"

"Let's get our drinks, and sit somewhere."
"Why, yes: if you think Kate wouldn't care—
I don't want the child to pull my hair!"

Queenie took cushions from the double bed.
"Do you mind if we sit on the floor?" she said.
So they found a corner
Half-hidden by a chair,
And they dropped the
     cushions,
And they sat down there.

Thought Black:
     "This is obvious bait:
She wants to be kissed.
Why wait?"

His arm went around her:
He whispered her name.
But Queenie was playing a different game.
She registered child-like dismay:
"No!—Please!" she gasped:
"Go away!"
She pushed him off: averted her head.
"I thought you'd be different,"
She said.

His arm dropped like a shot.

He choked

And his ears turned hot.

And he'd thought this woman a prostitute!

What a cad he was!

What a rotten brute!

He stammered:

"I'm awfully sorry!" he said:

"Just awfully—

Really!

I—lost my head.

Please forgive me?"

She lifted wet eyes.

She gave out the faintest of sighs.

Then bravely she winked the tears away:

Bravely she nodded:

She tried to be gay.

She smiled, wistful;

She pursed her lips,

And blew him a kiss from her finger tips.

His soul was torn.

It bled.

He wished to God he were dead!

Gloomily, he inspected his feet.

"You're the sort I've always wanted to meet,"
He said:
"And now it's spoiled.
You probably think I'm just hard-boiled:
A rotter:
A rounder:
A horrible sort of bounder!"

Queenie viewed him with large eyes,
Incredulous:
My God—what a prize!

"Well," he said: "I guess I'm through.
I'll go now, if you want me to."

Queenie shook her head.
She said:
"No—
Don't go.
You're really very nice, you know.
Please be my friend—
I need one so!"

His eyes lit with the pleasure
Of a man discovering treasure.
"There's nothing I'd rather be!"
He told her

Fervently.

Up rose his drink:

Up rose her drink.

The glasses met with a faint clink.

Glass met lip.

Each took a sip

To Friendship.

Meanwhile, on the double bed,

Eyes closed in bliss,

Burrs and Kate lay locked

In a five-minute kiss.

Of course —

It meant nothing to either one:

They were simply snatching a bit of fun.

They stirred:

They unlocked:

They came up for air.

Their eyes blurred:

The room rocked:

They peered here and there.

Suddenly Kate had a moving thought:

"Where's that cock-eyed bastard I brought?"

Her eyes found the corner,
And there they stopped.
Her head shot forward,
And her jaw dropped.
"Well!
May Jesus give me grace!
He's mushin' it up with your angel-face!"

"Yeah?" said Burrs.
He turned to look.
His eyes narrowed, and his hands shook.
"Yeah?" he said: "So they tell us!"

Kate winked slyly:
"You're jealous!"
"Jealous?"
He gave her a glittering stare:
"You're crazy!
What the hell do I care!"

The candles flared: the shadows sprang tall,
Leapt goblin-like from wall to wall;
Excited:
Delighted:
Mimicking those invited.

The noise was like great hosts at war:
They shouted: they laughed:
They shrieked: they swore:
They stamped and pounded their feet on the floor:
And they clung together in fierce embraces,
And danced and lurched with savage faces
That were wet
With sweat:
Their eyes were glassy and set.

On the bench before the grand piano
Sat Oscar and Phil; the brothers d'Armano.
They played with fury to the crowd about them:
Banged, and sang,
And tried to outshout them.

They swayed: they bent:
They hammered on the keys,
And shrieked falsetto melodies.

Now Jackie stood back of Phil,
And his hands just wouldn't be still!
One clutched Phil's shoulder:
The other was bolder:
It ran white fingers through his long black hair,
Then fondled his throat,
And rested there.

Phil's hands played on with agile grace,

But he leaned back:

Lifted his lily-white face.

Jack took it between pink finger-tips:

He bent down, and kissed Phil on the lips.

Oscar saw,

And his hands went *crash*

On the keys.

He leapt up like a flash.

His voice rose in a thin shriek:

"You kissed him!

I saw you—you nasty sneak!"

Phil raised his eyebrows:

"Well—what if I did?"

A groan from Oscar.

He sank down. He hid

His face in his hands.

He cried.

"There—there! " soothed Phil:

He embraced him;

He sighed.

But Oscar jumped up, tragic-eyed.

"Don't you dare touch me!" he shrilled:

"Don't touch me!

I'd rather be killed!

After all that we've been to each other,

You offer yourself to another!

My God! I can't bear it,

I swear it!"

The onlookers' views were varied and divided,

And they offered advice

To the one with whom they sided.

They grinned:

Egged them on:

Cheered: laughed: derided.

Finally Phil:

"Go to hell, then, will you?"

Cried Oscar: "Oh, you beast!—

I'll kill you!"

And he leapt on him, then and there.
They slapped:
They pulled each other's hair:
They sobbed, and panted:
Their faces grew smeared
With tears and mascara.
The crowd cheered:
Jeered.

But Jackie stepped forward:
He pushed in between.
"Look here," he said: "you're making a scene!"
Oscar turned on him, streaming-eyed:
"This is all your fault!" he cried.

"I know. Sorry. I didn't think.
Let's all get together, now,
And have a drink;
And be gentlemen, instead of boors:
And you'll sing us that nice new song of yours!"

After much persuasion, they were pacified.
They kissed;
They sat down side by side.
And Jackie rose
On the tips of his toes:
(How he kept his balance,
God only knows.)
He waved both hands to still the noise:
"Be quiet a minute, girls and boys!
The Brothers d'Armano—
(Stand up, boys: bow!)
Have a brand-new song;
And I'm sure it's a wow!
'My Sweetie is Gone,' is the new song's name.
They will now proceed to sing you the same!
And I know right now, it's going to be grand:
Now—!
Give these two boys a great big Hand!"

They cheered: they whistled:
They began to clap:
And Jackie sat down suddenly in Sally's lap.
The room stood waiting:
The room stood still.
In the hush,
    a woman laughed;
Drunken: shrill.

A chord rang out: turned blue, and ran

Through a syncopating vamp,

And the song began.

The verse was nothing—but the chorus was Art;

And its music was enough to tear you apart:

"My

Cuddlesome

Blond-headed-sweetie

Is

Gone !

(Doggone)

Oh!

How

I wish I had

Never been

Born!

(I told you, Born)

She had those

Kiss-me eyes

And lips—

What legs!

What a pair of hips!

I never had

A sweetie so bad—

So glad—

So sad—

She drove me mad!

O-oh—!

My

Adorable

Tow-headed cutie

Is gone!

(She left at dawn)

Get out your

Handkerchiefs,

Brothers and

Sisters and—

Mourn!

(I said to *M-m-mourn!*) "

The crowd went wild: they swore it a wonder!

They roared,

And stamped applause like thunder.

Even three couples who lay tight-clinched

On the bed

Stirred

A little as they heard,

And looked up to see if the place was pinched.

"Do it again!

Encore! Encore!"

The Brothers submitted.

Came a hush once more.

But just as Phil's fingers were about to light

On the keys, a voice came out of the night.

And the voice was angry,

Sepulchral,

Deep:

"Cut out that noise! I want to sleep!"

Silence

For a minute's fraction:

The silence of stupefaction.

Then they growled;

Howled:

They took action.

They swarmed to the window

Like a subway crush

Storming a train in the five o'clock rush.

They jostled:

Stepped on each other's toes:

Elbowed:

Clawed:

Their voices rose

In imprecations, fiercely applied.

They thrust grim, furious heads outside.

Night.

And against this night, the steep

Black neighboring walls

Shot up out of sight:

Sinister: silent:

Cold.

Asleep.

They peered up the slanting face of stone.

Across the gulf

A window shone:

Square: yellow:

And they shrieked—

"There's the fellow!"

A man's figure appeared,

Stood set

Against the light in silhouette.

Again the voice:

"Cut out that noise!"

"You bastard! Who the hell are you?"

"My god! It's only half-past two!"

"Pull in your neck!—"

"Go soak your head—!"
Were among the more polite things said.

"You're keeping decent people awake!"

"Aw, shut up! So's your Uncle Jake!"

"Decent?" roared Eddie.

"Yes—
Decent, I said!"
"Come here and I'll break your lousy head!
You cock-eyed son-of-a-bitching scut!
D'ye think you own this town, or what!"

"Yeah? I guess you're pretty tough!"
Said the voice, sardonic:
"Now, can that stuff!
I've asked you decently to stop—
If you don't,
I'm going to get a cop!"

"You can have your cop, you naughty boy!"
Shrilled Mae: and the others roared with joy.

"You heard me—!"
The silhouette disappeared.
The victors cat-called:
Hissed:
Jeered.

The light across the way went out.
They pulled in their heads.
They stood about.
They grinned.
With lurid epithets,
They said what they thought of silhouettes.
"He wants t' sleep, th' dear sweet bastard!"
Sneered Eddie: "That guy ought to be plastered!"

"You can have yer cop, see? I told him—"

"Yeah! Great stuff, kid; that'll hold him!"

"You piped him down, Mae!"

"Say, you're swell!"

"'Be quiet, youse—'!
Say!—
Let's raise hell!"

Burrs turned.
A group or two away
Stood Black and Queenie:
Intimate: gay.
He stopped: he eyed them.
For a minute, a mist seemed to hide them;
And Queenie's hand rose; made a white streak
Against the tan of the stranger's cheek.

Burrs' eyes narrowed.
His brows met.
The palms of his hands grew cold with sweat.
Then his eyes grew sharp:
Bored them.
He shouldered his way toward them.
"Queenie!"
She turned:

"Oh—hello, Burrs."
It was coolly delivered.
His mouth quivered.

"Queenie! Come here!"
She turned white.
"Just a minute," she said to Black:
"I'll be back."

She stepped aside with Burrs.
"Well—?"
Her tone was as hard as a steel bell.
His stare smouldered. His voice was rough:
"Lay off that stuff!"

"What stuff? What the hell do you mean!
Are you trying to make a scene?"
But her eyes glinted:
Her white cheeks tinted.
So Burrs
Felt the spurs!
Swell!
She'd give him a gaudy taste of hell!

"You know what I mean! Lay off that guy!"

"Why?"

"Because I tell you to!"

"Yeah?—And who the hell are you!"
A pause.

"Drop it!—It's the bad news!"

Flashed Queenie:
"I'll do what I damn well choose!"

"Not if I know it!"

He seized her wrist:
Gave it a twist.

She flinched,
And made a low wail.
Black stepped up:
He was ghastly pale:
He gave Burrs one knife-like glance,
Then turned to Queenie:

"Would you care to dance?"

Burrs watched them go with out-thrust head.
He sneered.
He joined Kate on the bed.

The candles flared: their flames sprang high:
The shadows leaned dishevelled, awry:
And the party began to reek of sex.
White arms encircled swollen necks:
Blurred faces swam together: locked
Red hungry lips:
Closed eyes:
Rocked.
White shoulders burst their ribbon bands;
Rose bare to passionate, fumbling hands:
White slender throats curved back beneath
Attacking mouths that choked their breath.

They murmured:
They gasped:
They lurched, and pawed, and grasped.

The bed was a slowly moving tangle
Of legs and bodies at every angle.
Knees rose:
Legs in sheer stockings crossed,
Clung: shimmered: uncrossed: were lost.
Skirts were awry.
Black arms embraced
White legs naked from knee to waist.

Madelaine True and the girl like a nun
Lay deep in cushions, locked as one.
Madelaine's uncovered shoulder shone
Through gun-metal hair, dully; like bone.
The girl's face was hidden: pressed
Deep in her slow, uneasy breast.

Dolores had broken her comb:
She wept to be taken home.
She shook off a shoe:
She pulled off a stocking:
A young man joined her,
And they sat there rocking.
They stared sadly at her scarlet nails.
The young man wept.
She burst into wails:
She hid her face on the young man's shoulder.
What could the young man do but hold her?
Her nails were his secret passion,
He told her.
She seemed to believe it.
They clung:
They kissed.
Shortly, they left together:
Unmissed.

The bedroom door swung open wide,

And a girl sauntered out

With a man at her side.

They kissed, in a matter-of-fact way,

And were mildly gay.

His suit was badly out of press.

She tried to smooth her crumpled dress

With small success.

He pulled his tie back in its place:

She rouged her lips:

She powdered her face.

She rearranged disordered hair.

What had been going on in there?

Everyone knew

Who noticed the two—

And nobody seemed to care.

Over blurred keys swung Oscar and Phil.

Their hands were numb:

They had lost their skill.

With faces ashen

And smiles set,

They played a duet.

Their fingers slipped:

Their fingers stuck,

Mangled the jarring notes they struck.

They clattered:

They rumbled;

The rhythm staggered and stumbled.

Through all this sound

The Victrola kept flinging

Dim snatches

That had no end,

No beginning.

Three couples circled

Slowly:

Clinging.

Backs to the room; sprawled on the floor,

Black and Queenie sat once more.

Drinks stood beside them.

They slouched at ease.

Her head rested on his drawn-up knees.

And this was all right—
Quite.
When people are sworn friends,
All carnal thought ends.
Sex is despised:
You'd be surprised!
So, then, they sat; and his fingers played
Gently with the blur her gold hair made.
From time to time, they would brush her cheek.
Once in a while, each would stare, and smile:
When the spirit moved them, they would speak.

Now Black looked her a soft, adoring kiss.
"It seems so queer—
Finding you here:
Like this.
It's wonderful."
He hesitated: shy.
"It's hard to say: I don't know.
You—
And I—
And all this noise back there—"
(A frown. A stare.)
"Perhaps all that's the world.
And we don't care.
Just being here together
Makes it seem

Unreal, somehow.
It's rather like a dream."

She nodded. She closed her eyes, and opened them.
Each eye was like a water-misted gem.
She sighed softly.
She smiled:
"You're a sweet child—"
With eyebrows raised,
She shook her head a little, as though amazed.

Again, he scowled: he took a longish drink.
"Don't think me rude—
You're marvellous, I think.
You're much too fine for what's around this place.
This Burrs, f'rinstance.
I'd like to smash his face!
Twisting your arm!
He's yellow, I'd like to bet!"

Fiercely he struck
A match for her cigarette.

Then Queenie gave him a queer look.
Her voice spoke, and her voice shook.
"When I first met Burrs,

He was grand—
You understand?
As nice as a man could be.
He was sweet to me.
I was sick, and awfully lonely,
And tired. I had no show.
And Burrs is the sort who pretends
He wants to be just friends.
I was only sixteen; how could I know?"
She shrugged:
"It seems ages ago."
Her mouth drooped.
Her lashes fell.
"You've no idea. I've been through hell.
What good does it do
To say I'm through?
Who have I got to turn to?"

Bravely she smiled,
Poor, battered child!
Tears filled his eyes to overflowing.
He turned his head
To keep them from showing.
He cleared his throat:
His eyebrows met:
"You've got me—always!
Don't forget."

"Dear boy!" she whispered.
Her finger tips
Rose in his hand, and met his lips.

From time to time, lying on the bed
With Kate, Burrs raised a dishevelled head
And scowled at blurred gold hair on a pair
Of wavering knees. The edge of the chair
Cut off the rest.
What went on there!
Burrs trembled:
He felt sick.
He ached for a bottle, a whip, a stick:
He'd batter that bastard green and blue
Before he was through!
And Queenie too!

"Lie still, Burrsie!"
Kate's hand pressed
His hot head back against her breast.

6

The candle flames stood stiff and tall:

And the shadows lay overlapped on the wall.

A candle guttered; its flame died:

The shadows rushed in from every side;

A sinister, swift procession,

Taking grim possession.

The noise dropped to a strange, jumbling,
Low-pitched sound, like distant mumbling.
Over this blur the Victrola threw
Incessant music, soft and blue.

Under the grand piano were curled
Oscar and Phil, dead to the world.
They sprawled like corpses.
Their pinched faces
Showed ghastly white in unrouged places.

"Everyone elsh's awful tight:
Yessir!"
Said Jackie.
"As f'r me, could drink all night.
Yessir!"
Said Jackie.
"Mix 'em, too! Gin, wh-whisky, wine—
Twenny-five, thirty—still feel f-fine!
Yesshir!"
Said Jackie.
"So wassha use drinkin'?
    Makesh me mad!
Makesh no different how many have had!
Noshir!"
Said Jackie.

His eyes blinked.

His eyes shut.

He mumbled something—

No one knew what.

His mouth opened,

   and his face grew haggard:

He lurched forward:

Swayed:

Staggered:

Put out a hand,

Found nothing to hold,

Sank to the floor

And passed out cold.

Nadine,

Mae's kid sister,

Vanished.

No one missed her.

Suddenly a scream shot out:

"No! No!"

Heads lifted, peered about.

Again the scream of fear:

"Mae!"

Mae leapt up, swaying.

Nadine lay
On the floor, half hidden by a man in grey.
Her slim legs kicked.
She tried to seize
Her skirt and pull it down to her knees.
Mae rushed forward:
"Eddie!"
But he was there already.

His hand swept down; his grip grew tight
On the man's neck. His knuckles showed white.
His shoulders heaved.
With one drag
He pulled the man up like a limp rag.
The man's head rolled from side to side:
He stared at Eddie, vacant-eyed.

"You bastard, you! Foolin' with a kid!"

Snarled Eddie: "I'll show yuh!"

And he did.

His shoulders swung:

His fist drew back,

Shot out,

Struck

With a dull smack.

Back went the man's head:

He spun where he stood:

He fell flat, and lay there,

His face oozing blood.

The bystanders murmured in awe.

Eddie thrust out his jaw.

A woman laughed:

His ear caught the sound:

He snarled.

Ducked his head,

Swung swiftly around.

"Who yer laughin' at, yuh tart!

I'll break yer god-damned face apart!"

His lips curled, and his fang-like teeth

Gleamed crooked and savage underneath.

His shoulders began to twist.

Slowly he circled each fist.

He crouched:

His eyes shone red:

Grimly he said:

"Foolin' with a kid!"

He scowled.

"Come on, you bastards!

Fight!"

He howled.

"I don't like yuh, an' I don't know yuh!

And now, by Christ, I'm gonna show yuh!"

Among those present were Queenie and Black.

They stood in the circle behind his back.

Queenie turned white.

She whispered: "Slopped!—

He'll kill somebody if he's not stopped!"

Black heard, and his muscles tightened.

Eddie advanced,

And the circle gave,

Frightened.

Black stepped forward.

With one hand he grasped

A slim, empty bottle.

The watchers gasped.

They waited,
Fascinated:
Suppose Eddie turned!
They held their breaths,
And their sharp eyes burned.

Black leapt:
The bottle glittered,
Flashed,
Crashed
On Eddie's head:
Smashed.

Eddie grunted. His eyes shut.
He sagged like a puppet
With its knee-strings cut.
His arms swung limp:
His face turned white:
He rocked:
Fell forward:
Went out like a light.

The watchers cheered:

They scattered for drinks.

But Mae leapt forward like an angry lynx.

She screamed.

She clawed.

She almost tore

Black's clothing off.

She sobbed:

She swore:

"You hurt my man! You bastard, you!"

Black held her arms: what else to do?

"Let go my arms, you cock-eyed swell!

Let go,

God damn your soul to hell!"

She wrenched free,

Struck him once, then fell

On Eddie's back:

Writhed like a snake,

And sobbed as though her heart would break.

At intervals she would caress

Poor Eddie's head:

Shriek he was dead.

Then little by little

   her sobs grew less:

Fainter and fainter:

They stopped.

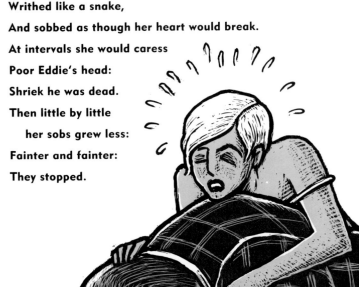

She sighed, and her head dropped.
Her eyes shut.
Her breathing grew deep.
Her lips parted,
And she lay asleep.

Burrs had been watching.
He stood there
With dishevelled hair:
Feet apart; shoulders stooping;
Hands in his pockets; head drooping:
Furious:
White:
His eyes had a glittering light.
Queenie joined Black:
They came his way.
Burrs stiffened, and his face grew grey.
They drew abreast; they made to pass
With cold shoulders and eyes of glass.
Burrs snarled.
He turned:
He tried
To shoulder Black aside.
But Black stood rigid: cut from rock;
And Burrs recoiled,
Staggered from the shock.
Then they passed on:

Not a word.
As though nothing at all had occurred.

Burrs raised clenched fists—
But his guts turned hollow.
He watched them go,
And he dared not follow.
He shook.
His face began to twitch:
"I'll fix you plenty, you son of a bitch!"

In a corner, a group well under the weather
Put arms across shoulders,
Thrust heads together.
With mournful voices, they howled that fine
Heart-rending song: "Sweet Adeline."
Their voices wailed from quavering throats
And clung fondly to the long, sad notes.
They swayed,
Leaned backward,
Closed their eyes
In sour attempts to harmonize.

7

Now,
Outside, in the night,
A window suddenly blazed with light.
The silhouette again,
About to complain!

But this time no sepulchral voice
Objected to the noise.
The shade stayed down:
Against its glow
A huge shadow moved to and fro.
The shadow sharpened,
Shrank,
Made
A clear black image on the shade.
In pantomime, a man was shown
Talking over a telephone.

8

Black took a drink as they passed the table:

A long one:

A strong one:

Then suddenly felt unstable.

The room blurred,

The room receded.

Another drink was what he needed!

So he poured it out, and he took it.

His head buzzed; and he shook it.

"Let's go sit," he suggested:

"Let's talk."

It became somewhat of a problem to walk.

They moved around the corner chair

With care.

He stumbled over a leg:

"I beg—"

He lapsed a second:

He shook his head,

Recovered:

"I beg your pardon!" he said.

Queenie's giggle was delicious,

Light.

"Oh, I'm all right,"

He said:

"Quite!—

But I think I must be tight!"

The words seemed out before he could speak:

They sounded far-off:

Strangely weak.

They both sat down in the usual place.

She arranged her skirt.

He pushed a rough hand over his face

Till it hurt.

There!

Now!

He felt much better.

He couldn't get drunk,

Having just met her!

With a sigh, she settled her head on his knees
And wriggled a little, till she felt at ease.
She smiled.
"Don't let's talk," she said:
"Let's be quiet for awhile instead."

So there was silence there.
His fingers played through her golden hair.
She closed her eyes.
Her head swirled.
Music came faintly from another world.
She forgot Burrs:

Her revenge grew dim.
This man wanted her,
And she
Him.
She had played: she had won—
But she was caught!
Her body ached madly at the thought.
What a man this was!
He seemed able to bring her
Heart leaping up with a touch of his finger.

She smiled
Like a child
In its sleep.

His hand left her hair.
It began to creep
With gently moving
    finger tips
Over her eyes:
Felt her lips;
Parted them:
Touched the perfect
    teeth
That lay underneath.

Lightly his hand began
    to float
Over the smooth white
    skin
Of her chin.
Then suddenly came
    to rest
With its palm pressed

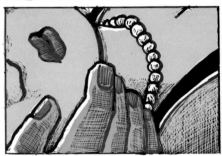

Soft and hot on the pulse
    of her slender throat.
She gave a sound like a sob.
Her body began to throb.
Some wire inside her broke
    with a snap,
And her head slid slowly
    to his lap.

For awhile, they were motionless:

Flushed:

Hushed.

Slowly the air about them became

Too thick to breathe:

Heated by flame.

Their hearts pounded till their brains shook:

Blood roared through their veins like a swollen
  brook.

His fingers ached

To feel fresh,

Cool flesh.

His hand waked.

It discovered her shoulders:

Began to explore

Under the edge of the gown she wore.

The edge of the gown was drawn taut

Across white flesh.

His knuckles caught.

The fingers began to retreat

In defeat.

Her head stirred in his lap.

She undid a shoulder strap.

Slowly his hand sank out of sight.

His heart pounded:

His throat grew tight.
His fingers fumbled at her brassiere.
It loosened.

He paused:
He did not dare.
Then his hot hand
Cupped her breast
Suddenly;
And came to rest,
Ecstatic: frightened.
But her hand covered his,
And tightened.
She gasped,
Started:
She flushed;
Her lips parted.
Unevenly her bosom lifted
And sank.
Her hand rose; it drifted
Light fingers slowly across his face.
Their breaths whispered:
They swirled in space:
And the soft, hot vortex of desire
Sucked them down
Gasping:
On fire.

His eyes opened. Through misty light
Her red mouth quivered in a blur of white.
Down drooped his head.
His breathing grew hoarse.
Suddenly
Their mouths leapt,
Met with a force
That bruised their lips; crushed them thin.
Their bodies stiffened;
And their cheeks sank in.

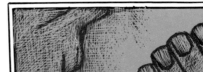

Tighter!
Tighter!
Their faces hardened,
Grew whiter.
Tighter!
Till every nerve and vein
Was shot with sharp, exquisite pain.
Sounds blurred:
The room began to sway.
Queenie tore her mouth away.
She gasped:
Buried her face in his breast.
For a moment, he held it there
Tight-pressed.

Then she raised her head and shook it.

She rose to her knees,

Put a hand out:

He took it.

They stood up, clinging:

They kissed.

They drew apart.

She took his wrist

And put that arm about her waist;

Then hers about his.

So, tightly laced,

They stood.

Her head dropped on his shoulder.

"I love you!" he told her.

She smiled dimly:

They kissed.

The room was hung with
    amber mist.

Exultant-eyed,

Side by side,

They floated dream-like
    across the floor

Towards the bedroom door.

No one stared:

No one cared.

Burrs—?
To hell with him!
As they passed the bed
She glimpsed his head
Face up,
White,
Dim:
Eyes closed;
Dishevelled of hair:
Mouth open:
Throat bare.

The door opened,
It closed behind them.
Jet-black darkness swept up to blind them,
And the air was strangely fresh and sweet.
They stood blinking:
They swayed on their feet;
And blank silence wrapped them in.
Little by little the dark grew thin.
A window glimmered with faint light:
The bed made a dim, soft blur of white.
They lurched forward,
Stumbled round a chair,
Staggered to the bed
And fell down there.

9

Some love is fire: some love is rust:
But the fiercest, cleanest love is lust.
And their lust was tremendous. It had the feel
Of hammers clanging; and stone; and steel:
And torches of the savage, roaring kind
That rip through iron, and strike men blind:
Of long trains crashing through caverns under
Grey trembling streets, like angry thunder:
Of engines throbbing; and hoarse steam spouting;
And feet tramping; and great crowds shouting.
A lust so savage, they could have wrenched
The flesh from bone, and not have blenched.

10

The studio flickered with uneasy light.

Two sunken candles made a fight

Against grim, overwhelming night.

Their flames flared,

Whirled up gyrating;

And a crowd of shadows hovered,

Waiting.

The curtains shivered with a sudden chill:

They stirred a little on the window sill;

Then billowed, and flapped inward
Blown
By a wind that smelled of damp stone.

The room was filled with a stale reek.
It looked dishevelled:
Sordid:
Bleak.
Figures sprawled out
Flat on their backs:
Their faces were death-masks
In dirty-white wax.

The table was a wreck.
Bleared glasses stood
Half-empty, bottoms stuck to wood.
Cigarette stubs:
Ashes:
Bits of bread:
Bottles leaning,
Prostrate;
Dead.
A pink stocking: a corkscrew:
A powder puff: a French-heeled shoe:
Candle-grease.
A dirty cup.
An agate saucepan, bottom up.

And a wet towel, with a stained border:
All stirred together in wild disorder.

Propped in a corner, two men stood giving
Each other a lecture on the high cost of living.
Horribly tight,
Equally polite,
Each insisted the other was right.
They stood there mumbling,
Gesturing, swaying:
Neither one knew what the other was saying.

The Victrola played steadily.
Beside it sat
A white-faced youth, with a battered hat
Aslant on his frowsy, dishevelled head.
Obviously, he wished he were dead.
He sat hunched over, staring at the wall
With eyes that saw no wall at all.
With half of one large foot he kept
The music's rhythm.
He wept.
The record played on.
Each time it ended,
He would look up startled: greatly offended.
He would then rise
With streaming eyes.

Carefully,

With a face of pain,

He would start the same tune over again.

The double bed was a tangled heap

Of figures interlocked; asleep.

Limp arms lay flung in all directions:

Legs made fantastic intersections:

White faces lay tossed back:

Mouth gaped; hideous, black.

Collars hung loose.

White bosoms lay bared.

One sleeper's eyes were open.

They stared

Up glassy; unfeeling;

At something beyond the ceiling.

A woman had taken off her gown.

She lay with drawn-up knees

In a heliotrope chemise.

Her flesh was tinted a delicate bronze-brown.

With his head hanging across Kate's knee,

Lay Burrs. He slept uneasily.

From time to time his body twitched

As though it itched.

Sleeping on her back, just next to them,

Lay a girl like a flower with a broken stem.

Her knees stood in the air.
From hip to knee, her legs were bare.
Her head rested in a pool of fair
Rippling hair.
Suddenly, she sighed:
Rolled over.
She clung to Burrs like a long-lost lover.
Burrs stirred: his legs shifted.
He moaned:
He groaned:
His head lifted.
He pushed the girl aside,
And sat up, crimson-eyed.

The room rocked.
Hammers knocked
Inside his skull.
It threatened to split.
None of his clothes seemed to fit.
His mouth and throat were foul cotton.
God, he felt rotten!

He writhed out to the edge of the bed
And sat there hunched;
Clutching his head.
But not for long.
Something was wrong!

Suddenly he had a thought.
His head lifted:
He grew taut.
He peered over at the corner chair,
Looking for knees, and blurred gold hair.
They were not there!

His throat grew tight:
His face turned white.
His eyes narrowed,
Vicious:
Suspicious.
Not so good!
He rose: he stood
Up aching,
Shaking.

He staggered to the corner,
Gripped the chair,
And peered behind it.
They were not there!

Two empty glasses,
Two pillows pressed flat,
Showed where Queenie and Black had sat.
A litter of ashes lay around them.
So this was the game!

God!
Wait till he found them!
He clamped his teeth together
And ground them.

His back straightened: he snarled: he wheeled.
Around and around the room he reeled;
Stooping; peering at white faces
That lay turned up in shadowy places.
Swifter and swifter he went:
Sinister: silent: intent.

At last he straightened.
He swore,
Baffled: whiter than before.
They were not there!
Then, where?

He went to the table to get a drink.
He must think!
He stared at the drink:
He stared at the floor:
He stared dully at the bedroom door
With eyes wide,
Blank.
His eyes swerved down:
He drank.

Then something moved in his brain.
His eyes shot up again,
And stared gleaming at the bedroom door
As though he had never seen it before.
Each eye suddenly narrowed to a slit:
His heart jumped.
So that was it!
He shook, and his ears rang.
He put down his glass with a bang.
His face was as white as though acid had bleached it.
Slowly he stepped towards the door:
Reached it:
Turned the knob:
Thrust the door wide:
Stood on the threshold,
And peered inside.

Dim light from the door
   streamed over the bed.
He saw locked figures,
And a golden head.
He felt sick.
His breath came quick.
The door shut behind him
   with a soft click.

Silence.

The pair on the bed

Sat up:

"Who's there?" Queenie said.

A black shape stirred near the door.

"Who's that?" sharper than before.

"Who the hell do you think?—

You whore!"

Silence.

Then, sharp; clear:

"Burrs—get out! Do you hear!"

"Get out like hell!"

His choking laugh:

"I'll break your god-damned neck in half,

You dirty bitch!"

His voice grew shrill.

Came Black's retort:

"The hell you will!"

Black rose:

The shadow sprang from the door.

Black struck:

Burrs reeled;

He crashed to the floor.

One hand reached slowly up to seize

The bureau's edge.

He got to his knees.

"Get up!" snarled Black

With his fist drawn back:

"I'll teach you to call that girl a whore!"

Silence.

In the darkness, a bureau drawer

Rattled:

Thumped.

Burrs thrust a hand in.

Up he jumped.

Something in his hand made a dull gleam.

"Look out!" shot Queenie's warning scream:

"Look out!—He's got a gun!

Look out!—"

Black made for him with a shout.

The gun roared—

But he missed.

Black caught him by the wrist.

He wrenched till the bones began to crack.

The gun dropped.

Black snatched it:

Stood up:

Lurched back.

The gun flashed—

Crashed!

Staccato,

    and vicious it spoke.

Silence.

Darkness.

The air smelled

    sharp with smoke.

Burrs stood stock still.

He whimpered faintly.

He cocked his head to one side,

Quaintly.

Suddenly he staggered,

Fell on the bed.

He groaned.

An arm rose—

Dropped.

He was dead.

"Burrs!" snapped Queenie,

Curt:

"Burrs!—Are you hurt?"

She leaned over;

Shook him;

Shrank back.

Her jaw dropped:

   she stared up at Black.

Then:

"Christ!—You've killed him!

Look what you've done!
Beat it, you fool!
Don't stand there—
Run!
If they get you
You'll get the chair!
Run!
Get out!
Take the gun:
Don't let them catch you with it!
Run!
D'ye hear?
Run!"

"Kiss me before I go!" he said.

Her hands flew up; beat at her head:

"God, what a fool!
You make me sick!"

"Kiss me!"

"All right, then—
Come on!—
Quick!"

110

For a moment, their lips met:
Cold; salty with sweat.

Feet trampled in the hall outside.

"What's that!" gasped Queenie,
Terrified.
He let go:
Turned:
Lurched towards the door
Through darkness, over a swaying floor.

A crash!—
The chair:
He almost fell.
"Chris'!" he mumbled:
    "what th' hell—?
Jes's Christ!—
    I've hurt my shin:—"

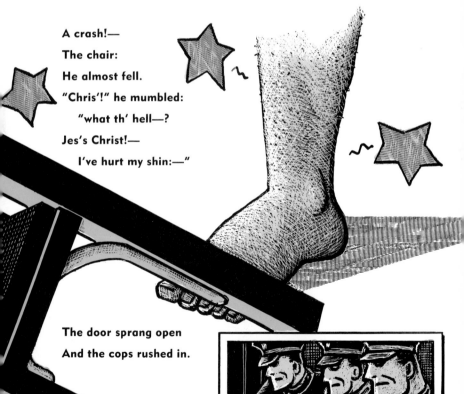

The door sprang open
And the cops rushed in.